Cinnamon

By Lou Seibert Pappas
Illustrations by Vivienne Flesher

CHRONICLE BOOKS

SAN FRANCISCO

Printed in Hong Kong.

Library of Congress Cataloging-in-Publication Data.

Pappas, Lou Seibert.
    Cinnamon by Lou Seibert Pappas;
  Illustrations by Vivienne Flesher
          p. cm.
    Includes index.
    ISBN 0-8118-0344-9
    1. Cinnamon. I. Title.
  TX819.P45P36   1994
  641.8'14–dc20   93-24860
                                         CIP

Cover design: Marianne Mitten
Composition: Marianne Mitten

Distributed in Canada by Raincoast Books,
8680 Cambie Street, Vancouver, B.C. V6P 6M9

10 9 8 7 6 5 4 3 2

Chronicle Books
275 Fifth Street
San Francisco, CA 94103

Cinnamon

———◆———

Acknowledgments

*My four children—Derek, Alexis, Christian, and Niko—
have instilled in me a love for cinnamon
through their enthusiasm over the years for the many
family favorites scented with this spice.
Susie Shelling Lopes, Peter Zimmer, and Lucretia Smith
each contributed a recipe idea from their culinary repertoire.
Ann Cinderey of Spice Islands shared historical lore,
and Cathie Colson perused the recipes with fine-tuned logic.
Carolyn Miller proved a delightful, meticulous editor.
Many thanks to all of you.*

Contents

Introduction

Cinnamon, that beloved traditional spice, evokes in me memories of early childhood. Mom's warm and fragrant cinnamon rolls, oozing with chewy caramel, first kindled my love for this captivating spice. Breakfast breads were dashed with a shake of it, and cinnamon toast, with its crackly broiled topping, was a comforting Sunday night ritual, along with fruit salad and hot chocolate bobbing with marshmallows.

Through the years, cinnamon has been a welcome taste and fragrance: in the streusel swirl of a chocolate bundt cake, in the crumbled topping for a cakelike apricot breakfast torte, and in the caramelized sugar glaze on spiraled yeast rolls.

Entrées take on a new dimension with the seductive power of cinnamon. A cherished family savory, a Grecian beef stew relies on a cinnamon stick and pickling spices to perfume the aromatic sauce. A versatile staple, cinnamon adds another flavor note to pastas, pita pockets, moussaka, and vegetables.

Around the world, cinnamon enhances Indian, Middle Eastern, and Eastern European savory dishes—tandooris, tagines, couscous, curries, pilaf, and strudels—and Mexican fare as well. Fruit and feta make an intriguing salad with a cinnamon-sparked dressing tying the ingredients together.

Old-fashioned desserts like baked apples, crème brûlée, and rice pudding wouldn't be the same without a hint of cinnamon, even when they get a contemporary update. Snappy brown sugar crisps, chewy hazelnut or chocolate macaroons, and chocolate chip cookies all are enhanced by its aroma. A delectable chocolate sponge nut cake and a fruit-and-nut carrot torte are other prize sweets with a touch of cinnamon.

Cinnamon holds an esteemed place in my kitchen. I hope you enjoy its alluring accent in these sweets and savories.

The History of Cinnamon

It tickles the tongue with its bittersweet intrigue; it tantalizes the taste buds. Once more costly than its weight in gold, cinnamon has been prized for eons—as far back as 2700 B.C. One of the earliest spices mentioned in Sanskrit texts and the Bible, cinnamon was used by the ancients as a body scent, an incense, and as a flavoring in wines. Its sweet, vibrant flavor later became essential in savory dishes both to mask and to impede spoilage, thanks to its antiseptic properties.

This age-old spice is made from the inner bark of a tropical evergreen tree. True cinnamon (*Cinnamomum zeylanicum*) grows only on the island of Sri Lanka and is mild and delicate in taste and pale tan in color. A member of the laurel family, the cinnamon tree has stiff, oblong green leaves and silky clusters of yellowish white flowers that mature into small, oval blue berries. Under cultivation, the trees are severely pruned to produce shrubby plants with many slender stems that contain a double bark. When the shoots are six to eight feet high, they are cut off during the rainy season, and the corky outer layer of bark is stripped away to obtain the aromatic inner bark. When dried, this bark curls and folds into itself, forming long quills that are cut and sold as sticks or ground into powder.

Most cinnamon sold in the West is really cassia (*Cinnamomum cassia*), also derived from a tree belonging to the laurel family. Pungent, slightly bittersweet and reddish brown in color, it comes from China and Indochina and is much less expensive than true cinnamon. In this country, no legal distinction is made between the two types, and often they are blended.

Long valued as a spice, cinnamon was acquired by the ancient Greeks and Romans from Arabian traders. Camel caravans plying the Silk Route from the Far East, and Arab ships sailing eastward with the monsoons and returning when the winds shifted, provided Rome with all its spices. The collapse of the Roman Empire was accompanied by a decline in shipping, and Europe was deprived of exotic flavorings until the Crusaders recovered the fragrances of the East in the twelfth century.

"It took the age of exploration and the discovery of the Spice Islands by the Magellan expedition to make cinnamon possibly the most widely used spice of Europe," writes Waverley Root in *Food*. During the Renaissance, cinnamon turned up in almost every Italian dish and became one of the most important seasonings in English cooking as well. The Dutch East India Company grew rich on spices, and its most profitable one was cinnamon. It was the Dutch who inaugurated the cultivation of cinnamon in the eighteenth century, for wild trees had supplied the demand until then.

Today, cinnamon is prized in cuisines around the globe. Indian curries, Moroccan tagines, Greek stews, Middle Eastern pastries, American fruit compotes and pies, breads, cakes, and cookies are dependent on its lively spiciness. Long prized in traditional American dishes such as apple pie, sweet rolls, steamed puddings, fruit crisps, baked apples, and spice cookies, cinnamon also fills a niche in new American cuisine, scenting granola, muffins, stews, chocolate tortes, and crème brûlée.

Storing & Using Cinnamon Sticks & Ground Cinnamon

Cinnamon sticks are popular flavor additions to chutneys, pickles, and jellies and are used to stir hot mulled wine and chocolate. The sticks or quills are also preferable in dishes where only a hint of cinnamon flavor is desired. Stick cinnamon has a long shelf life if kept in a cool, dry, dark place. Ground cinnamon deteriorates quickly and should be kept in airtight containers away from sunlight and replaced when the scent and taste decline in quality, about every year or two. For optimum fragrance and flavor, grind your own cinnamon: Break a stick into small pieces and grind it in a spice grinder, coffee grinder, or blender.

Breakfast Treats

Mexican Chocolate

Mexican chocolate with cinnamon sticks for stirrers makes a great brunch treat or breakfast drink. In Mexico, this drink is made with a chocolate bar that contains sugar, cinnamon, and ground almonds. Twirled into warm milk with a wooden molinillo, it explodes into frothy bubbles. Mexican chocolate is traditionally served in the afternoon with decorative sweet breads or sugar-coated fried churros, but it is also lovely in the morning with sugar-crusted cinnamon toast.

3 ounces bittersweet chocolate, cut into pieces
4 cups milk
1 teaspoon ground cinnamon
3 tablespoons firmly packed brown sugar
1 teaspoon vanilla extract
4 cinnamon sticks

Melt the chocolate in a small bowl placed over hot water. In a medium saucepan, warm the milk and stir in the ground cinnamon and sugar. Stir a small amount of milk into the chocolate to blend, return this mixture to the saucepan, and heat through. Add the vanilla and whisk until frothy. Pour into mugs and add cinnamon sticks for stirrers.

NOTE: For 1 serving, place in a pan or a mug $^3/_4$ ounce bittersweet chocolate, 1 cup milk, $^1/_4$ teaspoon ground cinnamon, and 2 teaspoons firmly packed brown sugar. Heat on top of the stove, or microwave on high for 1 minute and 40 seconds, or until heated through. Stir in $^1/_4$ teaspoon vanilla extract.

MAKES 4 SERVINGS

Cinnamon Granola

This favorite breakfast treat makes a great around-the-clock snack, or you can use it as a crunchy sweet topping for smoothies, fruit crisps, and frozen yogurt.

$^1/_3$ *cup firmly packed brown sugar*
$^1/_3$ *cup canola oil*
$^1/_3$ *cup honey*
$^1/_4$ *teaspoon salt*
2 tablespoons water

1 teaspoon vanilla extract
1 teaspoon ground cinnamon
4 cups old-fashioned rolled oats
$^1/_2$ *cup toasted wheat germ*
$^1/_3$ *cup roasted sunflower seeds*

OPTIONAL ADDITIONS
$^3/_4$ *cup golden or dark raisins, or* $^1/_2$ *cup diced dried apricots or diced pitted dates, or* $^1/_3$ *cup finely chopped candied ginger*

$^1/_2$ *cup (2 ounces) sliced almonds, chopped walnuts, chopped pecans, or coarsely chopped pistachios*

Preheat the oven to 300°F. In a small saucepan, place the brown sugar, oil, honey, salt, and water. Heat until the mixture comes to a boil and the sugar has dissolved. Remove from heat and stir in the vanilla and cinnamon. Place the oats in a large bowl and pour the liquid over them; mix to coat completely. Let stand for 15 minutes.

Spread evenly in a greased 10-by-15-inch baking pan. Bake on the middle rack of the preheated oven for 20 minutes, stirring once or twice. Stir in the wheat germ and sunflower seeds. Return to the oven and bake 10 minutes longer, stirring once. If desired, add the fruit and nuts and bake 10 minutes longer, or until golden brown.

MAKES ABOUT 6 CUPS

Whole-Grain Cinnamon Cranberry Muffins

An espresso and a big plump muffin from the enticing showcase of a Muffins shop in San Francisco inspired this recipe. The bakers there use an ice cream scoop to fill the pans with batter—a neat idea to duplicate at home. Fresh or frozen cranberries can be used interchangeably in these healthful muffins, which tally less than a gram of fat apiece but still exude a moist richness.

$^1\!/_2$ cup rolled oats
3 tablespoons oat bran
$1^1\!/_2$ cups whole-wheat flour
$^2\!/_3$ cup firmly packed brown sugar
$1^1\!/_2$ teaspoons baking powder
$^1\!/_2$ teaspoon baking soda
$^1\!/_2$ teaspoon salt
2 teaspoons ground cinnamon
1 egg
1 cup buttermilk
$^1\!/_3$ cup golden raisins
1 cup fresh or frozen cranberries or blueberries
$^1\!/_4$ cup chopped walnuts or pecans

Preheat the oven to 350°F. Place the oats and oat bran in a blender or food processor and blend or process until fine. Spread in a baking pan and bake for 8 to 10 minutes, or until lightly toasted. Let cool to room temperature.

Preheat the oven to 375°F. In a medium bowl, combine the flour, sugar, baking powder, baking soda, salt, cinnamon, and ground oat mixture. In a small bowl, whisk together the egg and buttermilk; pour this mixture over the dry ingredients and mix just until blended. Gently stir in the raisins, cranberries or blueberries, and nuts. Spoon into greased large (6-ounce) muffin cups, filling each one seven eighths full. Bake on the middle rack of the preheated oven for 20 minutes, or until golden brown. Remove from the pan to a rack. Serve warm.

NOTE: For a slightly moister muffin, if fat is no concern, add 2 tablespoons canola oil to the egg and buttermilk and proceed as in the basic recipe.

MAKES 8 MUFFINS

Cinnamon Sugar Spiral Twists

This European-style sweet roll is layered with a spicy sugar that melts into a candylike glaze during baking. The dough is particularly easy to handle and does not require kneading.

¾ cup (1½ sticks) butter, melted and hot
1 cup plain yogurt
¾ teaspoon salt
1 teaspoon vanilla extract

1 package (2 teaspoons) active dry yeast
1 cup sugar
2 eggs
3 cups unbleached all-purpose flour
2 tablespoons ground cinnamon

Pour the melted butter into a large bowl and add the yogurt, salt, and vanilla; the mixture should be lukewarm. Sprinkle in the yeast and 1 tablespoon of the sugar. Add the eggs and beat until blended. Gradually mix in the flour to make a soft dough; do not knead. Cover the bowl with plastic wrap and let rise at room temperature for 1 hour, then chill for 1 hour.

Mix together the remaining sugar and the cinnamon and sprinkle half of it on a pastry board. Roll the dough out into an 8-by 16-inch rectangle. Turn the dough in the sugar mixture to coat both sides. Fold in thirds, making 2 folds. Repeat the rolling, coating, and folding 3 more times. Roll into a rectangle about ¾ inch thick, 6 inches wide, and 15 inches long. Cut into strips ¾ inch wide and 6 inches long. Twist the strips several times while holding them at each end. Dip on both sides in the remaining cinnamon-sugar mixture. Place the twists 2 inches apart on a greased baking sheet. Cover with a towel and let rise in a warm place until light and puffy, about 1 hour.

Preheat the oven to 375°F. Bake the twists on the middle rack of the preheated oven for 20 minutes, or until golden brown. Remove from the pan to a rack. Serve warm or at room temperature. If desired, freeze; let thaw and reheat before serving.

MAKES 20 TWISTS

Sticky Cinnamon Rolls

A chewy caramel glaze coats the bottom of these light cinnamon rolls. This has been a beloved classic sweet roll in our family for three generations.

1 package active dry yeast
$^1/_4$ cup lukewarm water
$^1/_2$ cup milk
$^1/_4$ cup butter
$^1/_4$ cup sugar
$^1/_2$ teaspoon salt
1 teaspoon vanilla extract
2 eggs
$3^1/_2$ cups unbleached
  all-purpose flour

CARAMEL COATING
$2^1/_2$ tablespoons butter
$^2/_3$ cup firmly packed brown sugar
$^1/_4$ cup light corn syrup

CINNAMON FILLING
1 tablespoon melted butter
$1^1/_2$ teaspoons ground cinnamon
$^1/_3$ cup firmly packed brown sugar

In a small bowl, sprinkle the yeast into warm water and let stand until dissolved. In a saucepan, heat the milk and butter together until the butter melts. Pour into a large mixing bowl. Stir in the sugar, salt, and vanilla; let cool to lukewarm. Stir in the yeast mixture. Add the eggs, one at a time, and beat until smooth. Gradually mix in the flour, adding enough to make a soft dough. Turn out on a floured board and knead until smooth. Place in a bowl and cover with a towel. Let rise in a warm place until doubled in size, about $1^1/_2$ hours.

Prepare the caramel coating. Preheat the oven to 350°F. Place the butter, sugar, and corn syrup in a 9-by-13-inch baking pan and bake just until the butter melts and the mixture bubbles, about 7 minutes. Spread coating evenly over the bottom of the pan.

Turn out the dough on a lightly floured board and roll into a 10-by-12-inch rectangle. Spread with the melted butter and sprinkle with cinnamon and brown sugar. Roll up and cut into 1-inch slices. Place the slices in the caramel-coated pan, cover, and let rise until doubled in size, about 1 hour. Preheat the oven to 350°F. Bake on a rack in the middle of the oven for 30 minutes or until golden brown. Immediately turn upside down on a rack and lift off the pan. Serve warm or at room temperature.

MAKES 1 DOZEN

Chocolate Streusel Bundt Cake

Cinnamon-chocolate streusel forms a layered filling and topping on this fine-textured bundt cake that's been a favorite for decades.

CHOCOLATE STREUSEL
2 tablespoons butter
3 tablespoons unbleached
    all-purpose flour
1/3 cup firmly packed brown sugar
1 1/2 teaspoons ground cinnamon
2 tablespoons unsweetened cocoa
3/4 cup (3 ounces) chopped walnuts

1/2 cup (1 stick) butter at room temperature
3/4 cup granulated sugar
1 teaspoon vanilla extract
3 eggs
2 cups unbleached all-purpose flour
1 teaspoon baking powder
1/2 teaspoon baking soda
1/2 teaspoon salt
1 cup sour cream

To make the chocolate streusel: In a small bowl, mix together the butter, flour, sugar, cinnamon, cocoa, and nuts.

Preheat the oven to 350°F. Grease and flour a 10-inch bundt pan or tube pan. In a large bowl, cream the butter, sugar, and vanilla until light. Add the eggs and beat until smooth. Stir together the flour, baking powder, soda, and salt. Add to the creamed mixture alternately with the sour cream, blending until smooth. Turn half of the batter into the prepared pan, spreading it smoothly. Sprinkle with half of the chocolate streusel. Spread with the remaining cake batter and sprinkle with the remaining chocolate streusel. Bake on the middle rack of the preheated oven for 40 minutes, or until a wooden pick inserted in the center comes out clean. Let cool on a rack for 10 minutes, then turn out of the pan.

MAKES 12 SERVINGS

Apricot Caramel Coffee Cake

Spicy caramel cake batter puffs up between tangy apricots in this "oh so good" breakfast treat. Substitute other fruits of the season for year-round pleasure.

4 tablespoons butter at room
   temperature
$1/3$ cup firmly packed brown sugar
2 eggs, separated
$1/2$ teaspoon vanilla extract
$2/3$ cup unbleached all-purpose flour
1 teaspoon ground cinnamon
$1/4$ teaspoon salt
6 fresh apricots or plums, halved, and
   pitted, or 3 nectarines or pears,
    peeled, pitted or cored, and sliced

STREUSEL TOPPING
2 tablespoons firmly packed brown sugar
2 teaspoons unbleached all-purpose flour
2 teaspoons butter
1 teaspoon ground cinnamon
$1/3$ cup chopped or sliced almonds

Preheat the oven to 375°F. In a large bowl, cream the butter and brown sugar until light. Beat in the egg yolks and vanilla. Stir together the flour, cinnamon, and salt, and mix in. In a large bowl, beat the egg whites until soft peaks form and fold into the batter. Spread in a greased and floured 10-inch tart pan with a removable bottom. Arrange the fruit on top, cavity side up.

To make the streusel topping: In a small bowl, mix the brown sugar, flour, butter, cinnamon, and almonds until the mixture is crumbly. Sprinkle over the top. Bake on the middle rack of the oven for 25 minutes, or until the cake is crusty and the fruit is tender. Let cool on a rack or serve warm, cut into wedges.

MAKES 8 SERVINGS

French Cinnamon Galette

This pizzalike sweet bread is swiftly made and bakes in a flash. Serve it warm, short-cake style, with fresh berries and cream for a spectacular breakfast dish or dessert.

1 package active dry yeast
6 tablespoons warm water
4 tablespoons butter, softened
2 tablespoons sugar
1 egg
1½ teaspoons coarsely grated
   lemon peel
½ teaspoon salt
1⅔ cups unbleached
   all-purpose flour

TOPPING
2 tablespoons butter, softened
1 teaspoon cinnamon
3 tablespoons sugar

Mixed berries: raspberries, blackberries,
   and blueberries or sliced peaches or
   nectarines (optional)
Sour cream or berry-flavored frozen
   yogurt (optional)

In a large mixing bowl, sprinkle the yeast into the warm water and let stand until dissolved. Beat in the butter, sugar, egg, lemon peel, and salt. Gradually add enough flour to make a soft dough. Beat well with a heavy-duty mixer or wooden spoon. Turn out on a lightly floured board and knead until smooth and satiny. Place in a bowl and cover with a towel. Let dough rise in a warm place until doubled in size, about 1½ hours.

Punch down the dough and turn out on a floured board. Knead lightly. Roll out into a 15-inch circle and place in a greased 14-inch pizza pan or on a baking sheet. Form a rim around the edge. Spread with butter. Mix together the cinnamon and sugar and sprinkle over the top. Let stand in a warm place for 20 minutes to rise slightly.

Preheat the oven to 500°F. Bake in the oven for 6 minutes or until the crust is golden brown. Serve at once, warm, using scissors or a pizza wheel to cut it into wedges. If desired, accompany with berries or nectarines and sour cream or frozen yogurt.

MAKES 6 TO 8 SERVINGS

Spicy Nut-Swirled Coffee Cake

This spectacular yeast bread is remarkably easy to shape by snipping the coiled dough with scissors, then twisting and laying each slice flat, forming a decorative pattern.

2 packages (4 teaspoons) active
   dry yeast
$^1\!/_2$ cup warm (105° to 115°F)
   water
1 cup milk
6 tablespoons ($^3\!/_4$ stick) butter
6 tablespoons sugar
1 teaspoon salt
1 teaspoon vanilla extract
4 eggs
About 5 $^3\!/_4$ cups unbleached
   all-purpose flour

CINNAMON-NUT FILLING
$^3\!/_4$ cup (3 ounces) almonds or hazelnuts
$^1\!/_4$ cup sugar
2 teaspoons ground cinnamon
1 egg white

1 tablespoon butter, melted

Sprinkle the yeast into the warm water and let stand until dissolved, about 10 minutes. In a small saucepan, heat the milk and the butter until the butter melts. Pour into a large bowl and add the sugar and salt; let cool to warm (105° to 115°F). Stir in the yeast mixture and vanilla. Beat in the eggs, one at a time. Gradually beat in enough flour to make a soft dough. Turn out onto a lightly floured board and knead for 10 minutes, or until smooth and satiny. Place in a bowl, cover, and let rise in a warm place until doubled in size, about 1$^1\!/_2$ hours.

To make the cinnamon-nut filling: In a blender or food processor, grind the nuts with the sugar and cinnamon. Pour into a small bowl and blend in the egg white.

Turn the dough out onto a lightly floured board and knead lightly. Divide the dough in half. Roll one half into a 12-by-16-inch rectangle. With a spatula, coat this dough with half of the melted butter and spread with half of the cinnamon-nut mixture. Roll up the long side and place seam-side down on a greased baking sheet. Repeat with the remaining dough and filling. Cut through the rolls to within ½ inch of the bottom at ¾ inch intervals. Pull and twist each slice to lay flat, so that the slices lie alternately left and right. Cover with a towel and let rise in a warm place until doubled, about 45 minutes.

Preheat the oven to 325°F. Bake the coffee cakes for 30 to 35 minutes, or until golden brown. Remove from the pans to a rack. Serve warm, cut into 1-inch slices.

MAKES 2 COFFEE CAKES

Cinnamon Sugar Toasts

Chewy warm toast with a sugar and spice finish delights all ages.

8 slices sweet French bread, cut ½ inch thick
2 tablespoons butter, melted
3 tablespoons sugar
1 teaspoon ground cinnamon

Preheat the broiler. Place the bread on a baking sheet and brush each slice with melted butter. Mix the sugar and cinnamon and sprinkle evenly on the bread. Place under the broiler about 3 inches from the heat and broil until the top is golden brown, about 2 minutes.

MAKES 4 SERVINGS

Entrée Fare

Cinnamon-Spiced Fruit and Feta Salad

The sweet, spicy accent of cinnamon links fruit and cheese with greens in this refreshing salad plate. Arugula, with its peppery bite, is a vital ingredient. The dressing has become a staple in my kitchen. I blend it in quantity, store it in a tall slender bottle, and use it to dress greens and such fruits as Comice pears, Granny Smith or Fuji apples, and navel oranges.

SPICY DRESSING
2 tablespoons canola oil
2 tablespoons olive oil
1 teaspoon Dijon mustard
2 tablespoons raspberry vinegar
1 tablespoon dry white wine
1 teaspoon cassis syrup
1 shallot, chopped
1 teaspoon ground cinnamon
Salt and freshly ground pepper to taste

1 cup arugula or other bitter greens
   such as endive or watercress
3 cups mild-tasting greens such as butter
   lettuce, red oakleaf lettuce, and mâche
1 cup strawberries, hulled and halved
1 cup seedless grapes
3 ounces (3/4 cup) feta cheese, diced
3 tablespoons chopped pistachios or
   toasted pecans

To make the spicy dressing: In a small bowl, stir together the oils and mustard to blend. Stir in the remaining ingredients.

Place the greens in a large bowl, add the dressing, and toss to coat thoroughly. Add the berries, grapes, and cheese and mix lightly. Spoon onto salad plates and sprinkle with the nuts.

MAKES 4 SERVINGS

Chicken Tandoori

An Indian friend shared with me the trick of toasting the spices for this classic entrée. Pleasing accompaniments are spicy rice or couscous, and grilled eggplant, red peppers, and sweet onions.

¼ teaspoon saffron threads
1 tablespoon hot water
One 2-inch piece cinnamon stick
4 whole cloves
1 tablespoon coriander seeds
1 teaspoon cumin seeds
Seeds of 4 cardamom pods
1 small piece dried hot red pepper
1 cup plain yogurt
1 small onion, finely chopped
1 tablespoon chopped peeled fresh ginger
1 large garlic clove, minced
6 split chicken breasts, skinned, or one 3½-pound chicken, cut into serving pieces
Cilantro sprigs for garnish
1 lime, cut into wedges, for garnish

Soak the saffron in the hot water for several minutes until dissolved. In a small skillet over low heat, toast the cinnamon stick, cloves, coriander, cumin, cardamom, and dried red pepper for 10 minutes, shaking or stirring the pan frequently. Place in a spice grinder, blender, or food processor and process until finely ground. Add the yogurt, saffron and liquid, onion, ginger, and garlic, and blend. Place the chicken pieces in a bowl and pour the marinade over them. Cover and refrigerate for at least 2 hours or overnight, turning the chicken in the marinade several times. Remove the chicken from the refrigerator 30 minutes before cooking.

Grill over medium-hot coals or broil under a preheated broiler about 3 inches from the heat, turning to brown both sides and cook through. Allow about 10 to 15 minutes for the breasts and 15 to 20 minutes for the dark meat legs and thighs. Garnish with cilantro and lime wedges to serve.

MAKES 4 TO 6 SERVINGS

Chicken and Mushroom Strudel Rolls

Because they can be made ahead, these neat filo packets are an ideal entrée for a party or guest dinner any time of year.

4 large split chicken breasts (about 2 pounds total)
$^1/_2$ cup reduced homemade or canned low-salt chicken broth
$^1/_4$ cup dry white wine
2 tablespoons olive oil
1 small sweet onion, chopped
1 carrot, peeled and shredded
2 garlic cloves, minced
4 ounces mushrooms, sliced
2 eggs
2 cups (8 ounces) shredded regular or low-fat Jarlsberg cheese or Gruyère cheese
$^1/_4$ cup finely chopped fresh parsley
1 teaspoon ground cinnamon
1 teaspoon crumbled dried tarragon
Freshly ground black pepper to taste
10 sheets filo dough (about 13 by 17 inches each)
3 tablespoons butter, melted

Place the chicken in a large saucepan with the chicken broth and wine, and bring to a boil. Cover and simmer for 15 minutes, or until the chicken is opaque throughout; drain and let cool, reserving the broth.

In a medium skillet, heat the oil and sauté the onion and carrot until tender. Add the garlic and mushrooms, and sauté until glazed. Pour in $^1/_4$ cup of the reserved chicken broth and stir over medium heat to dislodge any browned bits on the bottom of the pan. Turn the mixture out into a small bowl and let cool.

Remove the skin and bones from the chicken and cut the meat into bite-sized pieces. In a medium bowl, beat the eggs and mix in the cheese, parsley, cinnamon, tarragon, pepper, sautéed vegetables, and chicken.

Lay out 1 sheet of filo (keep the remaining filo covered with plastic wrap), brush half of it with the melted butter, and fold the sheet in half, making a 9-by-12-inch rectangle. Brush again with butter and spoon about $\frac{2}{3}$ cup of the chicken mixture along the end of one short side. Fold in the long sides about $1\frac{1}{4}$ inches and roll up the filo, making a roll about $6\frac{1}{2}$ inches long and $1\frac{1}{2}$ inches wide. Place seam-side down on a lightly greased baking sheet. Repeat to use all the filo and filling. If desired, cover lightly with plastic wrap and refrigerate for 2 to 3 hours. Or, cover airtight and freeze; let thaw in the refrigerator before baking.

To bake, preheat the oven to 375°F and bake the rolls on the middle rack of the preheated oven for 15 minutes, or until golden brown.

Makes 10 rolls or 5 servings

Bastilla

The Moroccan entrée bastilla, with its bewitching aroma and sugar-dusted crust, is a show-stopper for a party dinner. Although it is time-consuming to prepare, it can be baked in advance, but it's best baked and served the same day. The word is also spelled bisteeya or bistayla, and denotes a pie of pigeon, squab, or chicken mixed with spices and nuts.

1 teaspoon olive oil
1 large onion, finely chopped
1½ teaspoons grated fresh ginger
1 teaspoon ground cumin
½ teaspoon each turmeric and allspice
2 teaspoons ground cinnamon
⅛ teaspoon cayenne pepper
One 3½-pound chicken
Salt and freshly ground black pepper
   to taste
¼ cup chopped fresh parsley

2 tablespoons chopped fresh cilantro
1 cup water
8 eggs
4 tablespoons butter
¾ cup (3 ounces) slivered blanched almonds
1 tablespoon granulated sugar
12 sheets filo dough (about 13 by
   17 inches each)
2 tablespoons sifted powdered sugar
About 12 blanched almonds

In a large saucepan, heat the oil and sauté the onion until it is translucent. Add the ginger, cumin, turmeric, allspice, ½ teaspoon of the cinnamon, and cayenne; sauté for 2 minutes, stirring. Add the chicken and brown on all sides. Season with salt and pepper, and add the parsley, cilantro, and water; cover and simmer for 1 hour. Remove the chicken from the pan and let cool. Remove the skin and bones and pull the meat into strips. Skim the fat from the broth, bring the broth to a boil, and cook to reduce it to 1 cup. Let cool slightly.

Preheat the oven to 325°F. Meanwhile, in a medium bowl, whisk the eggs until blended and stir in the reduced broth. In a large nonstick skillet, melt 1½ teaspoons of the butter, pour in the egg mixture, and cook, lifting from the bottom, until the eggs are just set but still soft and creamy; set aside.

Place the slivered almonds in a baking pan and toast in the preheated oven for 8 to 10 minutes, or until golden brown. Toss with the granulated sugar and $\frac{1}{2}$ teaspoon of the cinnamon. Melt the remaining butter.

Increase the oven temperature to 350°F. Brush a 14-inch pizza pan with the melted butter and place on it 6 sheets of filo 1 at a time, brushing each sheet lightly with melted butter and overlapping them to form a circle that extends over the edge of the pan. Sprinkle the filo in the pan with half of the toasted almonds. Cover with half of the egg mixture, then layer on the chicken and cover with the remaining egg mixture and the toasted almonds. Cover with 1 sheet of filo folded in to make a 14-inch square, then fold over the nearest sheet of filo from the bottom layer that extends over the edge of the pan. Repeat, placing the remaining 5 sheets of filo on top, brushing each one with melted butter and folding in the filo that extends over the pan edge. Brush the top with melted butter.

Bake in the preheated oven for 35 minutes, or until golden brown. Remove from the oven and place the pan on a rack to let cool for 5 minutes. Mix together the powdered sugar and remaining cinnamon, and sift over the top. With a knife, score through the sugar, making a crisscross pattern on top. Place 1 almond in the center of each square. Let cool slightly before serving. If desired, transfer to a board to present at the table and cut into wedges to serve.

MAKES 8 SERVINGS

Armenian Pizza Cartwheels

In this cross-cultural blending of global fare, plate-size flour tortillas are given a spicy meat and cheese topping for individual entrées.

2 teaspoons olive oil
1 small sweet onion, thinly sliced, or 4 green onions, chopped
1 garlic clove, minced
8 ounces ground turkey, lamb, or lean beef
1 teaspoon ground cinnamon
$\frac{1}{2}$ teaspoon ground allspice
1 tablespoon chopped fresh basil, or 1 teaspoon crumbled dried basil
1 tablespoon chopped fresh oregano, or 1 teaspoon crumbled dried oregano
2 tablespoons chopped fresh flat-leaf (Italian) parsley
Salt and freshly ground black pepper to taste
2 tablespoons pine nuts or pistachios
2 ounces feta cheese, diced ($\frac{1}{2}$ cup)
Two 10-inch flour tortillas
$\frac{1}{4}$ cup tomato paste
$\frac{1}{2}$ cup (2 ounces) shredded Monterey Jack or regular or low-fat Jarlsberg cheese

Preheat the oven to 425°F. In a small skillet, heat the oil and sauté the onion and garlic until tender, about 10 minutes. Place in a bowl with the meat and lightly mix in the cinnamon, allspice, basil, oregano, parsley, salt, pepper, nuts, and feta cheese.

Place the tortillas on 2 separate baking pans. Spread each with the tomato paste to within $\frac{1}{2}$ inch of the edge. Scatter the meat mixture over and sprinkle with shredded cheese. Bake for 8 minutes, or until the meat is browned and the edges are crisp.

MAKES 2 SERVINGS

Cinnamon-Spiced Taco Casserole

For a potluck or party dinner, assemble this sprightly Mexican-style casserole a day in advance. Apropos accompaniments are sangría, a guacamole salad, hot rolled tortillas, and a fresh pineapple, melon, and strawberry platter.

MEXICAN MEAT SAUCE
1 tablespoon olive oil
2 onions, finely chopped
One 2-inch piece cinnamon stick
1 pound ground pork
1 pound ground turkey
2 garlic cloves, minced
2 cans (8 ounces each) tomato sauce
2 tablespoons red wine vinegar
$^{1}/_{2}$ teaspoon ground cumin
$^{1}/_{2}$ teaspoon chili powder
$^{1}/_{2}$ teaspoon dried oregano
Salt and freshly ground black pepper
   to taste
1 can (1 pound) dark kidney beans,
   drained

1 package (6 ounces) small corn chips
2 cups (8 ounces) shredded Monterey
   jack cheese
2 green onions, chopped
1 bunch fresh cilantro, stemmed and chopped
$^{3}/_{4}$ cup plain yogurt or sour cream

To make the Mexican meat sauce: In a large skillet, heat the oil and sauté the onions and cinnamon stick until the onions are soft, about 10 minutes. Add the ground meats and sauté until browned, about 5 minutes. Stir in the garlic, tomato sauce, vinegar, cumin, chili powder, oregano, salt, and pepper. Cover and simmer for 30 minutes. Remove the cinnamon stick and stir in the beans.

Preheat the oven to 375°F if cooking the casserole now. Place a layer of corn chips in the bottom of a buttered 2-quart casserole. Sprinkle with one third of the cheese. Cover the cheese with half the meat sauce. Add another layer of corn chips, one third of the cheese, and the remaining meat sauce. Top with the remaining corn chips and cheese. (If desired, refrigerate the casserole at this point.) Bake in the preheated oven for 20 minutes (40 minutes, if refrigerated), or until heated through. Toss the green onions and cilantro together and make a border around the top of the casserole. Spoon the yogurt or sour cream into the center.

MAKES 8 TO 10 SERVINGS

Moussaka

This classic Greek entrée has countless variations. Eggplant, zucchini, potatoes, and mushrooms are appealing substitutes for the eggplant, or a combination of two or more vegetables can be used. The dish can also be baked in small eggplant shells, small soufflé dishes, or ramekins for individual servings.

MEAT SAUCE
1 tablespoon olive oil
2 large onions, finely chopped
2 pounds ground beef, lamb, or
   turkey, or a combination of
   2 meats
$\frac{1}{4}$ cup tomato paste
1 cup dry red wine
2 garlic cloves, minced
1 tablespoon ground cinnamon
1 teaspoon ground allspice
Salt and freshly ground black
   pepper to taste
2 tablespoons minced fresh parsley

2 large eggplants
$\frac{1}{4}$ cup olive oil

CUSTARD SAUCE
4 tablespoons butter
$\frac{1}{4}$ cup unbleached all-purpose flour
3 cups milk
4 ounces feta cheese, crumbled (1 cup)
Salt and freshly ground black pepper
   to taste
$\frac{1}{4}$ teaspoon ground nutmeg
4 eggs, beaten

$\frac{1}{3}$ cup fine dry bread crumbs
1 cup (4 ounces) freshly grated romano
   or Parmesan cheese

To make the meat sauce: In a large skillet, heat the oil and sauté the onions until soft, about 10 minutes. Add the meat and cook until browned and crumbly, about 5 minutes; drain any excess fat. Stir in the remaining sauce ingredients. Cover and simmer for 45 minutes, or until the sauce is thick and the flavors are blended.

Preheat the oven to 400°F. Slice the eggplants ¾ inch thick. Place on 2 well-oiled baking pans and coat both sides of the eggplant with the oil. Bake for 30 minutes, or until tender, turning once. Reduce the oven temperature to 350°F.

To make the custard sauce: In a saucepan, melt the butter and blend in the flour; gradually add the milk, stirring until thickened. Stir in the feta cheese. Season with salt, pepper, and nutmeg. Gradually whisk the hot sauce into the beaten eggs.

Arrange half of the eggplant in a greased 9-by-13-inch baking pan. Mix the meat sauce with the bread crumbs, and spread half of this mixture over the eggplant. Sprinkle with half of the grated cheese. Cover with another layer of eggplant and the remaining meat sauce. Spoon the custard sauce over the top and sprinkle with the remaining cheese. Bake for 50 minutes, or until set and lightly browned. Let stand for 10 to 15 minutes, then cut into squares.

MAKES 12 SERVINGS

ZUCCHINI VARIATION: Substitute 2 pounds zucchini for the eggplant. Slice the zucchini about ⅓ inch thick lengthwise or on the diagonal. Sauté in the olive oil until crisp-tender. Continue with the basic moussaka recipe.

POTATO VARIATION: Substitute 2 pounds potatoes, peeled and sliced ¼ inch thick, for the eggplant. Sauté in the olive oil or 4 tablespoons butter until golden brown. Continue with the basic moussaka recipe.

MUSHROOM VARIATION: Substitute 2 pounds mushrooms, washed and sliced, for the eggplant. Sauté in 5 tablespoons butter just until soft and glazed.

Dried Cranberry and Pistachio Couscous

A quartet of spices permeates couscous with an intriguing flavor in this swift-to-assemble side dish. Partner it with grilled lamb, ribs, fish steaks, or roast chicken.

1 small sweet onion, chopped
1 tablespoon olive oil
1 teaspoon chopped fresh ginger
$1/4$ teaspoon ground cinnamon
$1/4$ teaspoon ground allspice
8 threads saffron
$1/4$ cup dry white wine
1 cup homemade or canned low-salt chicken broth
$2/3$ cup couscous
3 tablespoons dried cranberries, golden raisins, or currants
2 tablespoons chopped pistachios or pine nuts for garnish

In a skillet over medium heat, sauté the onion in the oil with the ginger, cinnamon, allspice, and saffron, stirring until tender. Add the wine and broth, and bring to a boil. Stir in the couscous and cranberries, raisins, or currants; cover, remove from heat, and let stand 10 minutes.

To serve, divide among small custard cups, press down to pack the contents, and invert onto dinner plates. Sprinkle with nuts.

MAKES 4 SERVINGS

Lamb and Apricot Tagine

The delightful mélange of spices, honey, citrus, and nuts adds an intriguing mix of flavors to slow-cooked lamb. A tagine is a slowly simmered Moroccan stew, cooked in a shallow earthenware pot with a conical top.

1 tablespoon olive oil
1 large onion, coarsely chopped
2 teaspoons chopped fresh ginger
One 2-inch piece cinnamon stick
$1/8$ teaspoon ground turmeric
$1/2$ teaspoon salt
Freshly ground black pepper to taste
1 garlic clove, minced

$1^1/2$ pounds lamb stew meat,
  cut into $1^1/2$ inch cubes
24 dried apricot halves
1 tablespoon honey
$1^1/2$ tablespoons fresh lime or lemon juice
2 tablespoons chopped pistachios or
  toasted almonds
Cilantro sprigs for garnish
Lime or lemon wedges for garnish

Preheat the oven to 325°F. In a heavy pot, heat the oil over medium heat and sauté the onion, ginger, cinnamon, turmeric, salt, and pepper, stirring until the onion is tender, about 10 minutes. Add the garlic and lamb, and sauté until the meat is browned, about 5 minutes. Cover and bake for $1^1/2$ hours.

Add the apricots to the meat and bake 30 minutes longer, or until tender. Remove the cinnamon stick. Add the honey and lime or lemon juice to the pan drippings and heat, scraping up the drippings. Sprinkle with nuts and cilantro sprigs, and garnish with lime wedges to serve.

MAKES 6 SERVINGS

Lamb Curry with Condiments

A perfect make-ahead party dish! This curry is even better when prepared a day in advance so the flavors have a chance to mellow. Ring the serving dish with condiments and pass rice seasoned with saffron and cloves for a "sheik" presentation.

1 cup chopped onions
1 tablespoon olive oil
2 garlic cloves, minced
One 2-inch piece cinnamon stick
2 teaspoons chopped fresh ginger
1 tablespoon chopped fresh cilantro, or 2 teaspoons ground coriander
$\frac{1}{2}$ teaspoon each ground turmeric, cumin, and dry mustard
$\frac{1}{8}$ teaspoon cayenne pepper
Salt and freshly ground black pepper to taste
2 pounds lean lamb stew meat, cut into 1-inch cubes
2 tablespoons red wine vinegar
$1\frac{1}{2}$ cups homemade or canned low-salt beef or chicken broth
1 tablespoon cornstarch mixed with 1 tablespoon cold water
$\frac{1}{4}$ cup plain yogurt, or $1\frac{1}{2}$ tablespoons fresh lime juice
Assorted condiments: chopped pistachio nuts, chutney, red or green
   seedless grapes, flaked coconut, chopped green onions

In a large, heavy pot, sauté the onions in the oil until soft, about 10 minutes. Add the garlic and spices, and cook for 1 minute. Add the meat and cook to brown all sides, about 5 minutes. Pour the vinegar into the pan and stir over medium heat to scrape up any browned bits. Pour in the broth, cover, and simmer for 1½ hours, or until the meat is tender.

Remove the cinnamon stick. Stir in the cornstarch paste to thicken the juices and cook until bubbly. Stir in the yogurt or lime juice. Serve with bowls of condiments to spoon over the curry.

MAKES 6 TO 8 SERVINGS

Golden Pilaf with Browned Butter and Cinnamon

Redolent of the East, saffron-hued rice becomes a festive dish when scented with cinnamon and orange zest, dotted with golden raisins and pistachios, and splashed with browned butter.

$^1/_8$ teaspoon saffron threads
2 cups plus 2 tablespoons water
Zest of 1 orange, cut into fine shreds
$^3/_4$ teaspoon salt
2 tablespoons olive oil
$^1/_4$ teaspoon ground cinnamon
One 2-inch piece cinnamon stick
1 cup long-grain rice
2 cups shredded peeled carrots
$^1/_3$ cup golden raisins
2 tablespoons butter
$^1/_4$ cup chopped pistachios or toasted slivered almonds

Place the saffron in a small dish and cover with 2 tablespoons of the water; let stand for 10 minutes. In a small saucepan, simmer the orange zest with water to cover for 2 minutes; drain. In a large pot, bring the remaining 2 cups water to a boil and add the salt, 1 tablespoon of the oil, saffron and liquid, ground cinnamon, cinnamon stick, and rice. Simmer, covered, for 15 to 20 minutes, or just until the rice is tender. Remove the cinnamon stick and set the rice aside.

In a large skillet, heat the remaining oil, add the carrots and orange zest, and cook over medium heat, stirring, for 3 to 4 minutes; do not brown. Add the raisins and heat through. Add to the rice.

In a small saucepan, heat the butter until it bubbles and browns slightly, and pour it over the rice, fluffing it with a fork. Sprinkle with the nuts.

Makes 4 to 6 servings

Beef and Onion Stew

Lightly toasting the cinnamon stick imbues the meat with a marvelous flavor as it slow-cooks. This is a superb dish to make in advance and reheat for a party. Accompany with pilaf and a tomato and cucumber salad strewn with feta and Mediterranean-style olives.

1 tablespoon olive oil
2 pounds lean beef stew meat, cut into 1 1/2-inch cubes
One 2-inch piece cinnamon stick
Salt and freshly ground pepper to taste
3 garlic cloves, minced
1 1/2 teaspoons mixed pickling spice
3/4 cup dry red wine
3 tablespoons red wine vinegar
3 tablespoons tomato paste
1 tablespoon packed brown sugar
1 1/2 pounds small whole onions
2 tablespoons currants (optional)
3 tablespoons finely chopped fresh flat-leaf (Italian) parsley

In a large skillet, heat the oil and brown the meat on all sides with the cinnamon stick. Season with salt, pepper, and garlic. Place the pickling spice in a tea ball or tie in cheesecloth and add to the meat. Pour in the wine and add the vinegar, tomato paste, and brown sugar. Cover and simmer for 1 hour.

Peel the onions and cut a small cross in the root end of each to prevent them from bursting. Add the onions and optional currants to the stew and simmer 30 minutes longer, or until the onions and meat are tender. Remove the cinnamon stick and pickling spices before serving. Sprinkle with parsley.

MAKES 6 TO 8 SERVINGS

Desserts

Tuscan Baked Apples

Pine nuts and golden raisins lend a chewy sweetness to delicious baked apples. Choose a firm apple that will hold its shape, such as Rome Beauty, Pippin, or Granny Smith.

4 firm apples
2 tablespoons golden raisins
2 tablespoons pine nuts
2 tablespoons sugar
1 teaspoon ground cinnamon
1 tablespoon butter
$\frac{1}{3}$ cup fruity dry white wine
   such as Riesling
Heavy cream or half-and-
   half (optional)

Preheat the oven to 350°F. Peel the top third of the apples and core them. Place the apples in a baking pan and stuff the center of each with the raisins and pine nuts. Mix together the sugar and cinnamon, and sprinkle over. Dot with the butter and pour in the wine.

Bake for 30 minutes, or until the apples are tender when pierced with a knife. Or, cover the baking dish with plastic wrap and microwave on high for 10 to 12 minutes, or until the apples are tender. Serve warm with cream, if desired.

MAKES 4 SERVINGS

Cinnamon Crème Brûlée

A sweet with textures and flavors galore: Tap through the crackly caramel topping and spoon up the satiny cognac-laced custard with its captivating cinnamon scent.

> 2 cups heavy (whipping) cream, or 1 cup heavy cream and 1 cup half-and-half
> One 2-inch piece cinnamon stick
> 6 egg yolks
> ¼ cup firmly packed brown sugar
> 2 tablespoons Cognac or brandy
> About ½ cup brown sugar for topping

In a double boiler over simmering water, heat the cream and cinnamon stick to scalding. Remove from heat and let stand for 30 minutes for the cinnamon flavor to infuse. In a medium bowl, whisk the egg yolks until light and beat in the brown sugar. Pour in a little of the cream, stir to blend, and return to the double boiler. Cook over simmering water, stirring, until the custard is thick enough to coat a spoon. Remove from heat and stir in the Cognac or brandy. Immediately place in a pan of ice water to cool. Remove the cinnamon stick and pour into 4 small (6-ounce) soufflé dishes. Chill.

Preheat the broiler. Lightly butter a sheet of foil and place on a baking sheet. Spoon the ½ cup brown sugar into a sieve and, with the back of a spoon, push out 4 circles of sugar about ⅛ inch thick and 3 inches in diameter, or slightly smaller than the diameter of the soufflé dishes. Place under preheated broiler and broil just until the sugar melts and caramelizes, about 30 seconds. Let cool. To serve, slip a caramel disc on top of each custard.

MAKES 4 SERVINGS

Spiced Kahlúa Ice

This cinnamon-spiced coffee ice has a lively impact and an amazingly low calorie count.

1/4 cup firmly packed brown sugar
2 cups water
One 2-inch piece cinnamon stick
6 whole cloves
3 1/2 teaspoons freeze-dried instant coffee granules
1/4 cup coffee liqueur, such as Kahlúa
1/2 teaspoon vanilla extract

In a medium saucepan, place the sugar, water, cinnamon, and cloves. Bring just to boiling, remove from heat, stir in the coffee, and let cool. Pour through a strainer to remove the whole spices and stir in the liqueur and vanilla. Pour into a shallow 9-inch pan and freeze until solid, about 2 hours.

Transfer the mixture to a food processor or electric mixer and process until light and fluffy. Return the mixture to the freezer and freeze until solid, about 2 hours. To serve, let soften slightly and spoon into dessert bowls or parfait glasses.

MAKES 6 SERVINGS

Cranberry~Pear Cinnamon Crisp

At the Anasazi Inn in Santa Fe, this homey fruit crisp steals the show in the dessert line-up. The juicy tang of plump warm cranberries counters the sweet spiciness of pears layered under a granola topping.

1½ tablespoons honey
¼ cup firmly packed brown sugar
1½ tablespoons walnut oil or a mild vegetable oil
1½ teaspoons ground cinnamon
1 cup old-fashioned rolled oats
½ cup (2 ounces) walnuts or pecans, coarsely chopped
4 Bartlett, Anjou, or Bosc pears
¾ cup fresh or thawed frozen cranberries or blueberries
Vanilla ice cream, frozen yogurt, or whipped cream for topping

Preheat the oven to 325°F. In a small baking dish, combine the honey, 1½ tablespoons of the brown sugar, walnut oil, and ½ teaspoon of the cinnamon. Bake for 10 minutes. Add the oats and toss with a fork. Return to the oven for 25 minutes, stirring once or twice. Remove from the oven and stir in the nuts.

Increase the oven temperature to 350°F. Peel and slice the pears into a bowl. Add the cranberries or blueberries and remaining brown sugar and the cinnamon; mix lightly. Spoon into a greased 2-quart baking dish and sprinkle with the oatmeal mixture. Bake for 20 minutes, or until the fruit is tender. Serve warm with vanilla ice cream, frozen yogurt, or whipped cream.

MAKES 4 TO 6 SERVINGS

Cinnamon-Orange Nut Chews

Almost flourless, this unusual nut macaroon has a rich, chewy texture and a flavor triumvirate of cinnamon, orange, and caramel.

1¼ cups (6 ounces) almonds
1 egg
½ cup firmly packed brown sugar
1 teaspoon grated orange zest
1 tablespoon all-purpose flour or rice flour
2 teaspoons ground cinnamon
⅛ teaspoon salt
3 tablespoons granulated sugar

Preheat the oven to 325°F. Place the nuts in a shallow baking pan and bake for 8 to 10 minutes, or until lightly toasted. Let cool. Place the nuts in a blender or food processor and grind until fine.

In a large bowl, using an electric mixer or wire whisk, beat the egg until it is thick and pale, then gradually beat in the brown sugar. Mix in the orange zest. Stir together the nuts, flour, 1 teaspoon of the cinnamon, and salt. Add to the egg mixture and mix just until blended. Chill for 1 hour.

Preheat the oven to 325°F. Roll teaspoonfuls of dough into small balls about 1¼ inches in diameter. Mix together the granulated sugar and remaining 1 teaspoon cinnamon and roll each ball in the sugar mixture, coating it evenly. Place about 2 inches apart on greased baking sheets. Bake on the middle rack of the preheated oven for 10 minutes, or until lightly browned but still soft inside. Remove and let cool on a rack. Store in an airtight container.

MAKES ABOUT 16 COOKIES

Apple-Walnut Harvest Torte

A layer of cinnamon sugar cloaks this fruit- and nut-filled cake, and shredded carrots lace it with a moist sweetness. Bake this for an easy special-occasion dessert.

2 eggs
1 cup firmly packed brown sugar
¼ cup unbleached all-purpose flour
1 teaspoon baking powder
⅛ teaspoon salt
1 teaspoon vanilla extract
1 teaspoon ground cinnamon
¾ cup (3 ounces) chopped walnuts or pecans
1 cup shredded peeled carrots
2 apples, peeled, cored, and diced
1 tablespoon granulated sugar
1 teaspoon ground cinnamon
Vanilla ice cream, frozen yogurt, or whipped cream for topping

Preheat the oven to 350°F. In a large bowl, beat the eggs until frothy and beat in the brown sugar until light. Stir in the flour, baking powder, salt, vanilla, and cinnamon. Set aside 3 tablespoons of the nuts for garnish. Mix in the remaining nuts, carrots, and apples. Pour into a greased 9-inch pie pan. Mix together the granulated sugar, cinnamon, and reserved nuts and scatter over the top.

Bake on the middle rack of the preheated oven for 25 minutes, or until set and golden brown. Let cool slightly. Serve warm or at room temperature with ice cream, frozen yogurt, or whipped cream.

Makes 8 servings

Hazelnut~Brown Sugar Cinnamon Crisps

Wonderfully crisp and buttery, these caramel nut wafers have just a hint of spice.

$^3/_4$ *cup (4 ounces) almonds or filberts*
1 cup (2 sticks) butter at room temperature
1 cup firmly packed brown sugar
1 teaspoon vanilla extract
$^1/_4$ *cup sour cream*
2 cups unbleached all-purpose flour
1 tablespoon ground cinnamon
$^1/_4$ *teaspoon baking soda*

Preheat the oven to 325°F. Place the nuts in a baking pan and bake for 8 to 10 minutes, or until lightly toasted. If hazelnuts are used, rub the hazelnuts between paper towels to remove the brown skins. Chop the nuts finely.

In a large bowl, beat the butter and sugar until creamy, and mix in the vanilla and sour cream. Stir the flour, cinnamon, and soda together and mix into the butter mixture, beating until smooth. Stir in the nuts. Divide the dough in half and shape into rolls about 2 inches in diameter. Wrap in plastic wrap and chill until firm, about 1 hour. If desired, freeze the rolls at this point.

Preheat the oven to 350°F. Cut through the dough into slices about $^1/_8$ inch thick and place them about 1 inch apart on ungreased baking sheets. Bake on the middle rack of the preheated oven for 8 minutes, or until golden brown. Remove and let cool on a rack. Store in an airtight container.

MAKES ABOUT 6 DOZEN

Bittersweet Chocolate-Walnut Macaroons

These chocolatey gems are a prize party or tea-time cookie. At an outdoor buffet party, they make a big hit when served along with chocolate-covered caramel-nut ice cream bars.

6 ounces bittersweet or semisweet chocolate
2 egg whites
$\frac{1}{8}$ teaspoon salt
$\frac{1}{2}$ cup sugar
1 teaspoon ground cinnamon
$\frac{1}{2}$ teaspoon cider vinegar
$\frac{1}{2}$ teaspoon vanilla extract
$\frac{3}{4}$ cup (3 ounces) chopped walnuts or pecans

Preheat the oven to 350°F. Melt the chocolate in a double boiler over barely simmering water; let cool. In a large bowl, beat the egg whites and salt until foamy. Gradually add the sugar, beating until soft peaks form. Add the cinnamon, vinegar, and vanilla, and beat until stiff. Fold in the melted chocolate and nuts. Drop rounded teaspoonfuls about 2 inches apart onto greased baking sheets.

Bake on the middle rack of the preheated oven for 10 minutes, or until puffed and lightly browned on the edges. Remove and let cool on a rack. Store in an airtight container.

MAKES 2 DOZEN COOKIES

Spicy Fruit-Filled Crêpes

For a Sunday brunch or summer dessert, these delicate berry-filled pancakes provide a regal treat. For ease, make the crêpes in advance and reheat at the last minute.

CRÊPES
2 eggs
1 tablespoon sugar
$1/4$ teaspoon salt
$2/3$ cup milk
$1/2$ cup cornstarch or flour
1 teaspoon vanilla extract
1 tablespoon butter

FILLING
3 cups mixed berries: raspberries, blueberries,
  blackberries, or sliced peaches or nectarines
1 teaspoon cinnamon
2 tablespoons powdered sugar
Whipped cream, sour cream, frozen
  yogurt, or ice cream

In a blender or food processor, place the eggs, sugar, salt, milk, cornstarch or flour, and vanilla, and blend until smooth. Heat a 6-inch crêpe pan and add $1/4$ teaspoon of the butter. When it stops sizzling, pour in 2 tablespoons batter or just enough to cover the bottom of the pan, tilting to let batter run. Cook over medium heat until golden brown underneath and set on top. Turn out of the pan and repeat the process to make about 11 more pancakes, buttering the pan each time.

Preheat the oven to 300°F. Toss the berries or peaches with the cinnamon and sugar and spoon about $1/4$ cup of fruit down the center of each crêpe; roll up and place in a baking dish. Heat in the oven until warm throughout, about 5 to 10 minutes. Serve two crêpes to each person and dollop with cream, if desired.

MAKES 6 SERVINGS

Caramel-Oatmeal Chocolate Chippers

*Bittersweet bites of chocolate fleck these wonderfully chewy caramel drop cookies.
If you can find a bar of Mexican chocolate, it lends a delightful accent with its cinnamon
scent and crystals of sugar.*

> $^3/_4$ *cup (1$^1/_2$ sticks) butter at room temperature*
> $^3/_4$ *cup each granulated sugar and firmly packed brown sugar*
> *2 eggs*
> *1 teaspoon vanilla extract*
> $^3/_4$ *cup each unbleached all-purpose flour and whole-wheat flour*
> *1 teaspoon baking soda*
> *1$^1/_2$ teaspoons ground cinnamon*
> $^1/_2$ *teaspoon salt*
> *2$^1/_3$ cups old-fashioned rolled oats*
> $^1/_2$ *cup (2 ounces) chopped walnuts*
> *1 cup (6 ounces) finely chopped bittersweet chocolate or Mexican chocolate*

Preheat the oven to 350°F. In a large bowl, beat the butter and sugars together until creamy. Beat in the eggs and vanilla. In a medium bowl, stir together the flours, soda, cinnamon, and salt; add to the creamed mixture and beat until smooth. Stir in the oats, nuts, and chocolate. Using a small scoop about 1$^1/_8$ inches in diameter, scoop out small balls and place them 1 inch apart on greased baking sheets, or drop the dough from a spoon.

Bake on the middle rack of the preheated oven for 10 to 12 minutes, or until golden brown. Remove from the oven and let cool on a rack. Store in an airtight container.

MAKES 3$^1/_2$ DOZEN COOKIES

Candied Ginger Rice Pudding Supreme

Short-grain rice is preferred for this custardy pudding that's nicely sparked with candied ginger bits and a dusting of cinnamon.

> $^1/_3$ *cup short-grain rice*
> $^1/_2$ *cup water*
> *4 cups milk*
> *2 tablespoons honey*
> *One 2-inch piece cinnamon stick*
> $^1/_8$ *teaspoon salt*
> *4 eggs*
> $^1/_2$ *cup sugar*
> *1 teaspoon grated lemon zest*
> *1 teaspoon vanilla extract*
> *2 tablespoons candied ginger, finely chopped*
> *Ground cinnamon for sprinkling*

In a small saucepan, bring the rice and water to a boil; cover and simmer until the water is absorbed, about 5 to 6 minutes. Transfer to the top of a double boiler; pour in the milk and add the honey, cinnamon stick, and salt. Place the pan over simmering water, cover, and cook for 1 hour, or until the rice is tender.

Whisk the eggs until light and beat in the sugar and lemon zest. Pour part of the milk and rice mixture into the egg mixture and return to the double boiler. Place over simmering water and cook, stirring occasionally, until the custard thickens. Remove from heat and stir in the vanilla. Cool immediately by placing the pan in a pan of ice water. Remove the cinnamon stick. To serve, spoon into dessert dishes and sprinkle ginger and cinnamon on top.

MAKES 6 SERVINGS

Chocolate-Almond Cinnamon Cake

This delectable ground nut and chocolate sponge cake is superb cut into wedges and accompanied with berries and whipped cream.

4 ounces bittersweet or semisweet chocolate
1⅓ cups (7 ounces) almonds or hazelnuts, or a combination
5 eggs, separated
⅛ teaspoon salt
⅛ teaspoon cream of tartar
1 cup plus 2 tablespoons firmly packed brown sugar
1½ teaspoons ground cinnamon
1 teaspoon vanilla extract
¼ teaspoon almond extract
About 1½ cups strawberries or raspberries (optional)
Whipped cream or ice cream for garnish

Preheat the oven to 350°F. In a food processor or blender, process the chocolate until finely ground, then add the nuts and process until finely ground. Turn out into a bowl. In a large bowl, beat the egg whites until foamy, add the salt and cream of tartar, and beat until soft peaks form. Add 2 tablespoons of the brown sugar and beat until stiff, glossy peaks form. In another large bowl, beat the egg yolks until thick and lemon-colored, then beat in the remaining 1 cup brown sugar, cinnamon, and vanilla and almond extracts until the mixture is thick and pale.

Fold half of the nut and chocolate mixture into the yolks. Fold one third of the whites into the yolks to lighten them. Fold in the remaining nut and chocolate mixture, then gently fold in remaining whites. Turn into an ungreased 9-inch springform pan.

Bake in the preheated oven for 30 to 35 minutes, or until the top springs back when touched lightly. Remove from the oven and let cool upside down on a wire rack. To serve, remove the pan sides and cut the torte into wedges. Accompany with berries, if desired, and garnish with whipped cream or ice cream.

MAKES 10 SERVINGS

Table of Equivalents

The exact equivalents in the following tables have been rounded for convenience.

US/UK

oz=ounce
lb=pound
in=inch
ft=foot
tbl=tablespoon
fl oz=fluid ounce
qt=quart

Metric

g=gram
kg=kilogram
mm=millimeter
cm=centimeter
ml=milliliter
l=liter

Weights

US/UK	Metric
1 oz	30 g
2 oz	60 g
3 oz	90 g
4 oz ($\frac{1}{4}$ lb)	125 g
5 oz ($\frac{1}{3}$ lb)	155 g
6 oz	185 g
7 oz	220 g
8 oz ($\frac{1}{2}$ lb)	250 g
10 oz	315 g
12 oz ($\frac{3}{4}$ lb)	375 g
14 oz	440 g
16 oz (1 lb)	500 g
$1\frac{1}{2}$ lb	750 g
2 lb	1 kg
3 lb	1.5 kg

Length Measures

$\frac{1}{8}$ in	3 mm
$\frac{1}{4}$ in	6 mm
$\frac{1}{2}$ in	12 mm
1 in	2.5 cm
2 in	5 cm
3 in	7.5 cm
4 in	10 cm
5 in	13 cm
6 in	15 cm
7 in	18 cm
8 in	20 cm
9 in	23 cm
10 in	25 cm
11 in	28 cm
12 in/1 ft	30 cm

Liquids

US	Metric	UK
2 tbl	30 ml	1 fl oz
$\frac{1}{2}$ cup	60 ml	2 fl oz
$\frac{1}{3}$ cup	80 ml	3 fl oz
$\frac{1}{2}$ cup	125 ml	4 fl oz
$\frac{2}{3}$ cup	160 ml	5 fl oz
$\frac{3}{4}$ cup	180 ml	6 fl oz
1 cup	250 ml	8 fl oz
$1\frac{1}{2}$ cups	375 ml	12 fl oz
2 cups	500 ml	16 fl oz
4 cups/1 qt	1 l	32 fl oz

Oven Temperatures

Fahrenheit	Celsius	Gas
250	120	$\frac{1}{2}$
275	140	1
300	150	2
325	160	3
350	180	4
375	190	5
400	200	6
425	220	7
450	230	8
475	240	9
500	260	10

Equivalents for Commonly Used Ingredients

All-Purpose (Plain) Flour/Dried Bread Crumbs/Chopped Nuts

¼ cup	1 oz	30 g
⅓ cup	1½ oz	45 g
½ cup	2 oz	60 g
¾ cup	3 oz	90 g
1 cup	4 oz	125 g
1½ cups	6 oz	185 g
2 cups	8 oz	250 g

Whole-Wheat (Wholemeal) Flour

3 tbl	1 oz	30 g
½ cup	2 oz	60 g
⅔ cup	3 oz	90 g
1 cup	4 oz	125 g
1¼ cups	5 oz	155 g
1⅔ cups	7 oz	210 g
1¾ cups	8 oz	250 g

White Sugar

¼ cup	2 oz	60 g
⅓ cup	3 oz	90 g
½ cup	4 oz	125 g
¾ cup	6 oz	185 g
1 cup	8 oz	250 g
1½ cups	12 oz	375 g
2 cups	1 lb	500 g

Long-Grain Rice/Cornmeal

⅓ cup	2 oz	60 g
½ cup	2½ oz	75 g
¾ cup	4 oz	125 g
1 cup	5 oz	155 g
1½ cups	8 oz	250 g

Dried Beans

¼ cup	1½ oz	45 g
⅓ cup	2 oz	60 g
½ cup	3 oz	90 g
¾ cup	5 oz	155 g
1 cup	6 oz	185 g
1¼ cups	8 oz	250 g
1½ cups	12 oz	375 g

Jam/Honey

2 tbl	2 oz	60 g
¼ cup	3 oz	90 g
½ cup	5 oz	155 g
¾ cup	8 oz	250 g
1 cup	11 oz	345 g

Grated Parmesan/Romano Cheese

¼ cup	1 oz	30 g
½ cup	2 oz	60 g
¾ cup	3 oz	90 g
1 cup	4 oz	125 g
1⅓ cups	5 oz	155 g
2 cups	7 oz	220 g

Index